FOCUS ON MAMMALS

Animal Watch

Stephen Savage

Gareth Stevens
Publishing

**Please visit our website, www.garethstevens.com.
For a free color catalogue of all our high-quality books,
call toll free 1-800-542-2595 or fax 1-877-542-2596.**

Library in Congress Cataloging-in-Publication Data

Savage, Steven.
Focus on mammals / Steven Savage.
        p. cm. (Animal watch)
Includes index.
ISBN 978-1-4339-5990-5 (library binding)
1. Mammals—Juvenile literature. I. Title.
II. Series: Animal watch (New York, N.Y.)
QL644.2.S294 2011
597.9—dc22

                        2010049252

This edition first published in 2012 by
Gareth Stevens Publishing
111 East 14th Street, Suite 349
New York, NY 10003

Editorial Director: Kerri O'Donnell
Design Director: Haley Harasymiw

Printed in China
CPSIA compliance information: Batch #WAS11GS: For further information contact Gareth Stevens, New York, New York at 1-800-542-2595.

Contents

What a Difference!

Elephants look very different from shrews and pandas. However, they are all mammals and they share a number of features.

MAMMAL CHARACTERISTICS

- Mammals are warm-blooded.
- Most mammals' bodies are covered in fur or hair.
- All mammals have lungs to breathe air.
- Most baby mammals are fully formed when they are born.
- Mammal mothers feed their young on milk.

← The African elephant is the largest mammal living on land. It can be 10 feet (3 m) tall and weigh up to 6 tons.

← The tiny pygmy shrew is the smallest mammal. It is only 1½ inches (36 mm) long and weighs 0.05 ounce (1.5 g).

Some mammals are giants and others are small enough to sit in your hand. They may also be very different in shape and color. The world's largest mammal is the blue whale. One of the rarest mammals is the giant panda, feeding only on bamboo in its forest home in China.

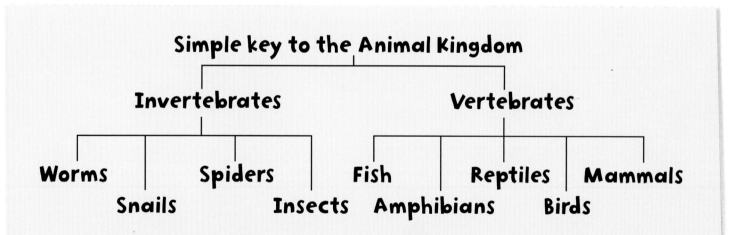

Simple key to the Animal Kingdom

Invertebrates   Vertebrates

Worms   Spiders   Fish   Reptiles   Mammals
   Snails   Insects   Amphibians   Birds

Invertebrates are animals that do not have a backbone.
Vertebrates are animals that have a backbone.

Where do mammals live?

Mammals live in all the world's important habitats. They are found in forests, grasslands, deserts, mountains, polar regions, rivers, and oceans.

↓ With their fishlike bodies, these spotted dolphins are able to live their entire lives in the sea.

↑ A giraffe can feed on the higher leaves of trees because of its long neck and legs. It can also spot predators a long way off and run from danger.

Mammals have special features that help them to live in these very different habitats. Monkeys living in the tops of trees have hands to grip branches and a tail to help them to balance.

MAMMALS AND DIFFERENT HABITATS

* **Many tree-living mammals never go down to the ground.**
* **Some desert mammals do not have to drink water.**
* **Some mammals dig burrows to hide from danger.**
* **Mammals living in cold regions have thicker fur in the winter.**

Catching the Meal

All mammals need food to live. However, the type of food and the way they eat can be very different.

↓ A tiger climbs down from rocks as it spots its prey.

AVOIDING DANGER

- Brown-colored antelope are hard to see.
- Opossums pretend to be dead to escape danger.
- Armadillos have tough, leathery armor on their bodies.
- Porcupine spines are 10 inches (25 cm) long.

↑ The aardvark lives in the African grasslands. It uses its sticky tongue to catch tiny termites for food.

Some mammals eat plants and others eat animals. Many use sharp teeth or claws to obtain their food.

↓ Humpback whales use their sievelike mouths to strain tiny food animals from the sea.

A few mammals use tools to help them catch their food. They use sticks to prize out insects from holes, and break the hard shells of nuts, eggs, or shellfish by banging them with rocks.

↓ A chimpanzee carefully pushes a twig into a termites' nest, then eats the termites that cling on to the end of the stick.

← Hedgehogs feed mainly on small animals and fruit. They curl into spiny balls if they sense danger.

Mammals that are hunted for prey often live together for safety. Some mammals have hard skin, prickly spines, or foul smells to protect them against predators.

↓ A skunk can defend itself against attack by squirting a foul-smelling liquid as far as 16 feet (5 m).

Hot and Cold

HOW TO KEEP WARM AND COOL

- Most mammals shiver to keep warm.
- Small baby mammals huddle together for warmth.
- Some mammals hibernate during the winter.
- Most mammals sweat to keep cool.
- Small desert mammals keep cool in their burrows.
- Elephants fan their ears to keep cool.

A mammal's fur or hair helps to keep it warm. In cold countries, mammals need very thick fur all year round.

The polar bear lives in the ➔ Arctic. It is the largest meat-eating mammal. Its thick white fur keeps it warm in the ice and snow.

Some mammals live in countries with hot and cold seasons. Their hair may be short in the summer and grow long and thick in the winter.

American bison grow a thick coat ➜ of hair for the winter.

↓ Whales, the world's largest mammals, have no fur. This 26-foot (8-m) killer whale is covered in thick blubber, which keeps it warm even in the coldest parts of the oceans.

Small mammals shelter in their burrows to keep cool on very hot days. Larger mammals move to the cool shade of a tree. Tree-climbing mammals find shady branches to keep them cool.

⬆ This squirrel lives in the scorching African desert. It uses its tail as a sunshade.

⬇ A muddy pool is perfect for keeping a Cape buffalo cool on a hot day.

Bathing in a quiet stream or a mud pool, or having a dip in the sea, are good ways of staying cool.

↑ Hippos spend 18 hours a day in water to keep themselves cool.

↓ This Hawaiian monk seal keeps itself cool on a hot beach by going to sleep.

Getting Around

Most mammals use all four legs when walking or running. They walk when traveling slowly and run to go faster. Kangaroos walk on all four legs but they use their back legs to make huge leaps when escaping from danger.

MOVING AROUND

- The cheetah is the fastest land mammal.
- The three-toed sloth is the slowest moving mammal.
- Dolphins swim and steer with their flippers and tail.
- Sea lions use flippers to walk and swim.

↓ When a Thomson gazelle runs at full speed, only a cheetah has a chance of catching it.

Mammals that climb trees have a tail that helps them to keep their balance. Kangaroos have tails to help them balance when they are bounding away from danger.

The three-toed ➔ sloth lives in the South American rain forest. It grips tree trunks with its curved claws. It moves very slowly.

← Bats have large, leathery wings. These are formed from their very long front legs and toes.

Bats are the only mammals that can fly. However, there are several mammals that are able to glide through the air.

Sugar gliders live → in Australian forests. They have a flap of skin between their front and back legs, which help them glide from one tree to another.

There are some mammals that only swim in water to catch food. Other mammals live in water all the time. They have a fishlike tail and flippers.

Sea lions use their front flippers like paddles for swimming. The back flipper is used for steering.

Mammal Young

All newborn mammals are cared for by their parents. Some are born blind and helpless, while others can walk soon after birth. Mammal babies feed on their mothers' milk.

⬆ Baby rabbits are born blind and helpless in the safety of their burrow.

Some types of mammals live in large groups. The young are still fed by their mothers, but they will be protected from danger by the whole group.

FACTS ABOUT YOUNG MAMMALS

- Baby monkeys cling to their mothers' fur.
- Baby dolphins are born in the sea.
- A newborn African elephant weighs 254 pounds (115 kg).
- Baby elephants need 9 gallons (34 L) of milk a day.

↓ A newborn wildebeest can walk with its mother and the rest of the herd just 15 minutes after birth.

↑ A lioness teaches her cubs what they will need to know to survive on their own.

Some mammals that live in groups, such as meerkats, share the care of the young. They may even have nurseries and babysitters.

← A female meerkat will take care of the young of another female while she goes hunting.

Most mammals are fully formed at birth, but some change throughout their lives. A few females have babies that grow in a special pouch. Some, like the echidna, lay eggs.

A baby kangaroo spends 300 days in its mother's pouch. Only one is born at a time.

Mammal Pets

Look closely at pet mammals such as cats or dogs. You will see that in some ways they are quite similar to wild mammals such as tigers and wolves.

Rabbits can be kept in a hutch. ➜ There should be a dark section with straw so that it is like a wild rabbit's burrow.

↓ Dogs are related to wolves, which live in a group. This is why dogs enjoy the company of humans.

HOW TO TAKE CARE OF YOUR PET MAMMAL

- Provide a cage or somewhere for it to sleep.
- Give it the right food and plenty of water.
- Remember all mammals need exercise.
- Keep the pet's cage clean.
- Most mammal pets enjoy company, so they shouldn't be left alone for long periods.

↓ Hamsters have a cheek pouch for storing food to eat later.

If your cat or dog has babies, you will see how mammal parents look after their young. You must not touch them or get too close.

Unusual Mammals

Some mammals seem very strange. They appear to have extra features added or others missing. Mole rats, for instance, have no hair at all and never leave their underground tunnels, where they feed on plant roots.

↑ The Australian duck-billed platypus uses its large flattened bill to pick up food from the bottom of rivers.

- Very large eyes and ears for finding food at night.
- Webbed feet for swimming.
- Long arms for swinging through trees.
- A tail that acts like an extra hand.

Other mammals have extra large features to help them live in difficult conditions. For instance, the elephant's trunk helps it to get water from deep underground.

But of all the mammals in the world, perhaps humans are the strangest.

Tarsiers have special toe pads for ➔ gripping branches. They hunt at night for insects and small animals.

Unusual Mammals

| Adult human | African elephant | Giant panda | Monkey | Spotted dolphin | Giraffe | Bengal tiger | Chimpanzee |

| Adult human | Polar bear | Cape ground squirrel | Californian sea lion | Blue whale |

| Adult human | Domestic cat | Dog | Gray wolf | Platypus | Hawaiian monk seal | Common echidna | Giant anteater |

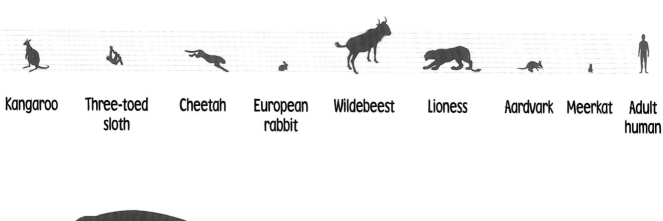

Kangaroo | Three-toed sloth | Cheetah | European rabbit | Wildebeest | Lioness | Aardvark | Meerkat | Adult human

Humpback whale | Striped skunk | Thompson's gazelle | Opossum | Nine-banded armadillo | Porcupine | Adult human

Pygmy shrew | Mouse-eared bat | Common hamster | Naked mole rat | Sugar glider | Tarsier | European hedgehog | Adult human hand

Topic Web

SCIENCE

Comparison of human features with features of other mammals.

How mammals adapt to their environment.

Food chain.

Growth and reproduction of mammals.

MATH

Measurement and comparison of mammal sizes with each other and with humans.

GEOGRAPHY

Mammal habitats.

Position of different habitats on a world map.

ENGLISH

Write a diary entry—"a day in the life of" a chosen mammal.

DRAMA/DANCE/MUSIC

Improvise to show movement of mammals.

Create music to illustrate mammal sounds.

ARTS & CRAFTS

Make a mural or collage showing a mammal or mammals and its/their habitat.

Design camouflage patterns.

Activities

Science Look at the similarities and differences between you and other mammals. What features are the same? What features are different? How do these features help mammals to survive? Make a chart showing a food chain.

Geography Look up the main deserts, rain forests, and grasslands in an atlas. Draw a simple world map showing these habitats and which mammals live in them.

Arts & Crafts Use art materials to make a mural of different mammals. Use camouflage patterns to make a design.

English Choose a mammal and write a story about it. Where does it live?

What does it eat? How does it move around? What dangers does it face?

Drama/Dance/Music Create a piece of drama or dance to show how different mammals move. Use music to help express the movement of different mammals. For example, deep, slow music for an elephant and fast, bouncy music for a kangaroo.

Math Measure yourself with a tape measure. Then, using the scale on pages 28-29, draw a chart to show how many mammals are bigger than you and how many are smaller.

Glossary

Arctic The region at or around the North Pole.

Armadillo A small animal covered with bony plates like body armor. It lives in Central and South America.

Blubber The fat of whales and other sea mammals.

Burrows Holes dug in the ground by rabbits, foxes, and other animals for shelter.

Camouflage Protection from attack by appearing to be part of the surroundings.

Habitat The natural home of a plant or animal.

Hibernate To spend the winter in an inactive state resembling sleep.

Invertebrates Animals that do not have a backbone or spine.

Opossum A tree-living marsupial.

Polar regions The areas around the North and South Poles.

Predator An animal that hunts others for food.

Prey Animals that are hunted and killed for food.

Termites Antlike insects living in large colonies.

Vertebrates Animals that have a spine or backbone.

Warm-blooded Refers to mammals whose body temperature stays about the same and is warmer than the surrounding air temperature. The skin may become hotter or colder, but the body temperature does not change.

Finding Out More

Books to Read

National Geographic Little Kids First Big Book of Animals by Catherine D. Hughes (National Geographic Children's Books, 2010)

Animals Called Mammals by Bobbie Kalman and Kristina Lundblad (Crabtree, 2005)

The Kingfisher First Animal Encyclopedia by John Kirkwood and John Farndon (Kingfisher, 1998)

Websites

National Geographic Kids
http://kids.nationalgeographic.com/kids/animals/creaturefeature/
Click on Mammals to learn all about these fascinating creatures and their habitats.

National Wildlife Federation
http://www.nwf.org/Wildlife/Wildlife-Library.aspx
Check out this web site to discover how your favorite mammal lives. You can also find out which animals live in your area!

Index

Page numbers in **bold** refer to photographs.

Picture Acknowledgements:
Bruce Coleman Ine. 4, /Andrew Purcell 5, /Jeff Foott Prod. 6, /Mark Boulton 7, /Jeff Foott Prod. 9(lower), /Peter Davey 10, /E. & P. Bauer 11(lower), /Steffan Widstrand 12 and title page (inset), /D. & M. Plage 13(top), /Bruce Coleman Ine.13(lower), /William Paton 14(lower), /Leonard Lee Rue 15 (top and title page, main pic) /E. & P. Bauer 15(lower), /Staffan Widstrand 17, /Jane Burton 20, /P. Van den Berg 21, /Eckart Pott 22(top), /John Cancalosi 26, /Sula Wesi 27; FLPA /Foto Natura cover (inset), /Gerard Lacz 8; NHPA /Roger Tidman 11(top), /Nigel Dennis 9(top) 14(top l.), 16 /Roger Tidman 14(top r.), /Stephen Datton 18(top), /A.N.T. 18(lower), /Norbert Wu 19, /Anthony Bannister 22(lower) and contents page; Shutterstock, cover picture, Tim Flach 12; Wayland Picture Library 24(both), 25.